FREEZING

New Issues Poetry & Prose

Editor	Herbert Scott
Associate Editor	David Dodd Lee
Advisory Editors	Nancy Eimers, Mark Halliday, William Olsen, J. Allyn Rosser
Assistants to the Editor	Rebecca Beech, Marianne E. Swierenga
Assistant Editors	Erik Lesniewski, Carrie McGath, Lydia Melvin Adela Najarro, Margaret von Steinen
Copy Editor	Diana Allen
Editorial Assistants	Derek Pollard, Bethany Salgat
Business Manager	Michele McLaughlin
Fiscal Officer	Marilyn Rowe

New Issues Poetry & Prose
The College of Arts and Sciences
Western Michigan University
Kalamazoo, MI 49008

First Edition, 2001

ISBN: 1-930974-06-X (paperbound)

Library of Congress Cataloging-in-Publication Data:
Langan, Steve
Freezing/Steve Langan
Library of Congress Catalog Card Number: 2001131165

Art Direction:	Tricia Hennessy
Design:	Haleem Rasul Ar-Rasheed
Production:	Paul Sizer
	The Design Center, Department of Art
	College of Fine Arts
	Western Michigan University
Printing:	Courier Corporation

for Giselle (Giz),
With memories of
you in your blue Camaro,
and with love + all
best wishes!

FREEZING

Steve

STEVE LANGAN

New Issues

WESTERN MICHIGAN UNIVERSITY

For Liz

Contents

IV

Acknowledgements

Chicago Review: "The Black Pants" (Days 1-7)

Colorado Review: "Freezing"

Columbia: A Journal of Literature and Art: "Poem Beginning with a Line from James Merrill"

Crab Orchard Review: "The Politics of Marriage"

Cutbank: "Tag"

DoubleTake: "Oceanic"

Flyway: "Artistic," "Manx"

Green Mountains Review: "Morning Poem"

The Greensboro Review: "Epithalamium"

The Journal: "Taxonomy"

The Kenyon Review: "Driving into the Unbeautiful City"

Many Mountains Moving: "Evangelical"

Midwest Quarterly: "Still Life in a Hanger with a Lion and a Woman," "In addition to terrors of absence, what's in the margins, the *white space*?"

The Nebraska Review: "Barkeep," "Industrialism," "Not My Body; Your Body"

Poet Lore: "Gossip"

Poetry Northwest: "Dinner Poem"

Rubber City: "Accidental Gunshot Wound"

Southern Humanities Review: "Genealogy Room, Omaha Public Library"

Witness: "Omaha"

I would like to thank the Copernicus Society and the James Michener Foundation for their support and funding.

This is the Hour of Lead—
Remembered, if outlived
            —Emily Dickinson

I

Driving into the Unbeautiful City

Driving into the unbeautiful city
gutters fill with rainwater and empty
the unbeautiful city rained upon

like an unbeautiful girl running home
in the rain under the dead half-moon
blouse torn from her shoulder

hard skin clawed from her shoulder
all of the city's industry coughs
its grain elevator rusts

Driving into the unbeautiful city
at night from the south
driving a cherry 1965 Ford Mustang

candy-apple red, newly waxed
or driving a rusted, skeletal pickup
a vehicle used to haul manure

and the long seedlings of grass
Driving into the unbeautiful city
drunk and worried about radar traps

squinting at slashes of white line
like an archer's distant bull's-eye
or sober right at the speed limit

whistling with pop tunes on the radio
Driving into the unbeautiful city
for dinner in its best restaurant

your reservations are at eight
the man you must meet speaks only Italian
Driving into the unbeautiful city

in the backseat in cuffs and leg irons
you give the marshal wrong directions
to the penitentiary south of town

an old man who spilled milk down your chin
and held a smoke to your lips like a lover
Driving into the unbeautiful city

for the first time
concerned about the apartment you rented
over the phone, the price very reasonable

the family dog falls asleep on your lap
you spill cold coffee on your crotch
your kids decide to have a spitting contest

Driving into the unbeautiful city
from the south you pass the labyrinth
of stockyard pens and walls and walkways

cattle out in the downpour snuffle at
men who work on the killing floor
smoking on their break in the wind and rain

men who mix brilliant red with brilliant red
their gadgets whirr, tools of death
high tide comes somewhere and it's blood

a place where you know no one and no one
knows you, the bloody tide arrives
at twelve-thirty P.M. and midnight

Driving into the unbeautiful city
blood gurgles in the dozen drains
on the killing floor

a worker sweeps hunks of skin from the drains
on the floor, it's a bloody waltz
it's midnight, love-hate overtime

the silver machinery roars
Driving into the unbeautiful city
your partner sleeps beside you

a friend or lover, it doesn't matter
the one who drives half the time
who began driving when your trip began

when you locked your empty apartment
in the south, blessed walls you punched
in angry blazes, said farewell to your sunrise

view, always on time and unclouded
Driving into the unbeautiful city
your partner snores through a violent dream

Driving into the unbeautiful city
with only a quarter-inch of brake left
streets slick as a rink, tires bald

but you wouldn't know that
following the arrows, clipping off miles
squinting at signs in the rain

finding no light in the city's shadows
no celestial light, no beacon, no portent
Driving into the unbeautiful city

Morning Poem

Lucky me, I have no memories of war.
I haven't wakened in a puddle of urine this decade.
"Whoever says the next cliché will be tortured"—
that's what I said, why I ended up here.
Most of all, I like to arrive a few minutes
before post time, the form under my arm,
and play my usual numbers. Which makes
those mornings a wade through unused strategy.
When they're in the stretch and I'm searching
for crimson-clad three I know the roar
of the crowd is stenciled on my bones.
There's also the story of the morning Doug-Bug
and I sat with his mother's thirty-eight between us,
which she had left either full or empty
depending on the state of the neighborhood.
But that's another story. Which to go into
would take away from the beauty and simplicity
of the birds at my birdbath with more than one
feeding through each slot of the cylindrical
birdfeeder I received as a gift. *Starlings?*

Freezing

No, I did not have to freeze that winter
in Kearney, Nebraska, where I lived yards
from the rail of the Second Avenue Bridge,
climbing out there nude to dizzying traffic,
and the girls I took home with me did not
have to freeze either, though they stayed,
just off farms. Maybe I reminded them
of their fathers, waking for harvest,
confusing their names, then pacing three rooms
with my coffee, no food there for them.
I dedicate this to the one who made me leave
one morning because she needed her juice.
I must have needed her warmth that badly,
but walking back, I began hating her the most,
the only one I can remember. May she live
as she decides, though she'll leave trails
of lust and possibility if she decides.
OK, Mother, I'll say it so they'll know:
I did not have to freeze that winter.
Sickness did not have to enter those rooms.
You would have sent me money to hook up
that ugly brown heater, mean bear, sleeping.
So that monkeys on motorbikes can deliver
these words to apes in charge, and elephants
tangled in cobwebs will stop their punishing
for a moment to listen, and especially one boy
in Upper Michigan who still has a chance,
who swims with every nude photo he's seen
in the bunk above his little brother, asleep,
the only one who may ever care about me,
so he will know I did not have to freeze
or break down in sickness, so he can tell
his mother, or his mother's gravestone,

that it was not your fault, that you would have
sent the money to buy me warmth. I feel
I must confess you were a good mother.
you brought me up in danger for a purpose,
drove me back to a fight I lost, blood
on my cheeks and elbows, and left me with
that boy who would do no more to me.
I did not have to freeze. Not for you.
I did not freeze for the sins I lived.
My wife, she says, "What if everyone we ever
slept with came over? Who would still love us?
Who would come to murder us?" And especially,
though she does not say it, "Who made successes
of themselves?" I thought you should know, Mother.
I am your only son. Sickness entered that cold.
Mother, you were a good mother. Make sure
you set your glasses on the night table before
you drift to sleep. I did not freeze for you,
Mother. Flower. Now. Time. Sleep. Please. Fire.

Barkeep

I still don't know that guy's name,
the one in the checked blazer
who calls me pal,

his taxi arrives, he leaves me
a word for a tip, glass
full of ice I flick

like hot dice then wash
in the electric washer that cleans all

but the lipstick the rare woman
leaves. Too many nights
to ask how far his fare goes,

what padlocked room he enters,
a boarder, or if that big house
on the hill is his.

I make the action: slowly,
or in the din of Friday evening,
factory checks fanned in front

of men. When they ask, I nod.
If they beg, this is how I pour:
bottle vertical, bubbling

a little extra, splashing
like sudden rain on the rooftop.

I put that bottle back in the rack
with a click.

I hold another dusty bottle up in the light.

After I rub the elbow stains
off the bar and the ashes
from the stack of chipped ashtrays,

I walk home
through the dark parking lot,

change musical in my pocket
loosening and fading white,

and when I throw it all down
on the table next to where

Elizabeth waits, sleeping,
it shines like a blade.

Throwing Glasses at the Wall

1
The first one fit in my palm,
a highball,
ice in its bottom dissolved, almost,
so ice was glass-like not melted hollow
when it hit the wall and did not soar but landed.
I almost want to say these are
the requirements to and after rage.
I want to find that middle, and rename it.
I think of finesse when I think of glass;

2
I think of speed, of accuracy.
Asleep atop Mt. Washington,
I know a man who was struck by lightning.
His big toe was exposed. The lightning entered
there "like getting my toes licked," he said.
His companions were frightened, and they left
down the mountain in the morning.

3
My hand could become glass
in some other, future life, my whole body
awaiting its command.
If my heart were glass not bloody muscle
I could run away from all of this.
There would be a place for me.

4
Why was I throwing glasses at the wall?
The wall was white, the room empty—just me.
There was music, annoying from the other rooms,
like relatives whispering
about my life, their lives, my life and theirs.

About one of them dead or one of them dying,
about one working one begging one stealing
to buy a few breaths.

5
The second glass was a champagne:
stolen love-prop, like a woman's slender body,
her long legs tapering, her thin-boned feet.
Lip over stem, its hatchet-cries cut the air.
My eye is all slow-motion now: it slows the crash.
Maybe this is a manual for rage,
but you bought yours, you wrote yours,
and when you painted yours
did its paint in your left hand resist loudly?

6
If you're playing alone at night,
and since you said you contain the wind,
is your metal and wood piano liquid, too?
And the third, the fourth, the fifth glass—
who cares . . . just glass for an instant in the air,
slamming, landing . . . (becoming enamored
of myself, on the mound, squinting, aiming, winding up).
Out there past the aiming field
was some nocturnal wilderness birds and fish ruled,
the rule you must fly and swim like we do.

7
—And the neighbors slept and dressed in the morning.
I hated wilderness and common sense. I hated
ideas and the affluent. I was not young;
I was not old. Too young and too old
to throw glasses at the white wall.
—The only picture was a horse and its rider.

8
Mighty horse, fearless rider.
The rider loved his horse, his horse her rider.
It was obvious.
I hated sentimentality, its glories and shame.
On one white tack, the drawing hung.
The wall was less white than it once was:
it was backstop; it was like memory.
In cabinets I found all that was glass that I owned.
I threw everything that was mine and glass.

9
If the horse and its rider were thirsty
and needed to drink,
have your drink, then ride and gallop.
Look to the west: the sun crudely rendered
in gold spokes is still the sun.
Here is your drink: thank me now.
I'll watch you gallop away
and appear as if I'm not watching.
—The next day I swept and bought
new glasses, twenty-four assorted in the box.

10
If the horse and its rider were tired,
riding through many days,
and they needed to rest,
it would be stupid for them not to rest—
but not here in my wilderness.
I have handed you water in the form of ice
and I have waited for you to drink,
which, today, is enough.

11
It is raining here
and the loud pretty fires in the sky
are burning kisses that in sleep resist shape.
The snarling dogs out there shouldering fences
are the same barking dogs who live
next door to me everywhere.
I walk by them through shadows
like a man displaying he has no weapon.
It would be easy to say I threw
those glasses for a reason: it was a game.

It is not raining in the west.
Gallop.
It's not raining near the setting sun.

Here is your water; here; *here.*
It is not raining where you are going.
I promise. *Here.*
Now *ride.*

Omaha

City no one's said it best about;
city that ignores its river,
its young, its elderly, its myths.

I sat in its taverns for five years,
my pledge not to miss a day—
that pledge got me nowhere,

no perched bar to lean on, elbows
dug in like roots, where I could watch
its river spill mighty waste sent down

to join its hostile older sister,
the Mississippi. For five years
I searched for the perfect tavern

like Ponce de León. The two rivers
meet in St. Louis, Missouri,
then spill into the Mississippi Delta

I have never traveled to see,
though I imagine it blue-green and lovely,
an infinite wishing well.

Omaha, no slogan worth repeating,
its storied horsetrack crumbling,
the three-year-olds winless—

I hate that town, I love that town,
I said, "Never going back . . . "
I promised to return only if

the bad gods who plagued me for years,
who chased me through its northside
streets, promised to sit quietly

in a dark room and listen to
my instrument rev and shudder,
and promised, after I finished,

to rise from their chairs, open
the windows and let that music out,
let in the cool north wind . . .

I've often dreamed of being revered
in Omaha, my hometown, by my neighbors,
who hated everyone.

It's where I learned fear trailing
out of dark, fenced homes:
blue flicker of TV, bodies through

the curtains like rounder blue shadows.
I would never allow them to bury me
like Mozart, thrown in with the paupers.

I would never let the bad gods take
that much of my body with them.
William, young son, please bury me

near traffic so I can listen
to cars pass, tremors of engines.
Visit, but not too often. Don't bring

bouquets: bring the songs you will
hold back from the world.
After all, William, who could love

a city that doesn't build good taverns
on its lovely river?
I would rather die in the fierce wind,

in winter, in a blizzard, rather than die in
the city named by an Indian chief—
O-ma-ha—who must have thought,

leading his weary tribe along
the curved edge, stopping for the night,
setting up camp, wandering off alone

to examine the glimmering and dark
patches, "Which direction from here
is my dream of a perfect landscape?

Bare fields, barefoot children, buffalo . . ."

Tag

1
On my side of the fence there's a pile
of weeds and roots like a dead dog's coat.
Dried leaves take flight, crash in the corners.
Starving raccoons ignore my trash.
The scar on my back is who I no longer am.
Just because I'm not strong doesn't mean
I wouldn't be useful as far as moving your piano.
I know finesse, technique, how to approach.
I'm certain it can be done by three of us.
It will fit in that empty corner, or that one.
My scar is not holy; it's not a design
of the orbit of any planet. I deserved it.
I prefer the dark—to forget all my lies—
you'll see the scar when the time is right—
I'll switch on the light, keep it on—
you might trace it with your long fingernail
again, or your tongue—you might turn away.

2
The neighbor boys and girls play
Kick the Can later than I can stay up.
They whisper and curse through my dream
of escape, they unlatch the gate, they hide
in my trees, the can rings off the curb,
they scuttle to safety, free.
While you trace the ribbon on my back
I'd like you to also kiss the scar on my shoulder:
I'll lie, you'll kneel, the TV on saying
end it all and join us now and improve
yourself, the remote in your free hand,
your eyes on the screen, mine on the ceiling.

3

—Just so long as you never utter we are planets
with divergent orbits, or you're my wishing-star,
or I'm your faithful moon.
The black dog chained to the metal toolbox
in the yellow Chevy's bed is not my demon.
Nature loves a Tarzan in her trees.
Does Tarzan think his hands vine to vine?
What do we do when our programs end:
sit propped in bed and listen to nature's squall
and children who one day will hope to die?
I'm stumbling a little, I'll be okay, I'm okay.
You've probably fallen into your deep sleep
that sounds like pain. If I eat, I'll sleep.
Inside my fridge a country of beggars sleeps.
In my cupboards, behind the row of soups,
I hide all the important documents.

Genealogy Room, Omaha Public Library

1
This room like a home frightens me.
Even the dusty tomes are liver-spotted.
A faint odor, like menhaden blended at sea,
riding high tide's spumes, on their clothes,
under their arms. I'm young, afraid
to mention things I've seen—not horrors,
just things only I have seen. Inept
at storytelling, unable to instruct
the old who bother me, silently,
for answers to questions certain to outlive
my children's children.

2
It's as if they face a last flight
of stairs, elevator out of order,
grocery bags unraveling in wilted arms.
Their numb forefingers follow the lines
in books heavy with dates,
eyes deep in skin like oiled mitts.

3
I won't be there soon,
where they'll rejoin their lost,
flowers at the edge of a foreign doorway.
A crowded place, waiters spin through
a ballroom with heaving trays of drinks,
music soars—"Any requests?"
the bandleader asks.

4
But I want to reassure them, though I fear,
to touch them the way I pat my children

into a cavern of sleep: *There is no Bogeyman.*
The branched oak is not witch-hair.
The library warning sounds: Everyone out.

5
No Bogeyman, no witches—Now sleep . . .

6
All of the time I've wasted with maps,
memoranda extracts, diaries, memories,
photos lost to time. Immeasurable time
lost in this room. I talked to no one,
no one interesting enough to die young.

7
When I discover my Irish surname
once had a jolly O attached,
like an arrow-through-heart tattoo,
warning-red, blazed on the mighty bicep
of this unforgettable night,
the band strikes up and plays

in the key a thousand jubilant throats
muster. Like statues hammered into form,
now the black-tie crowd lifts champagne high,

toasting to health, to life.

Terrarium

Instructions read *peer into the opaque sheets*
at the fruit in the planter but all I see on vines
are raisins. Or is it the stray hairs in my eyes,
all those subtle concussions, unrecorded?
I have no debt. I asked for no glorious life.
The rest of us—in their evening clothes,
drink and Bev-Nap—they can be forgiven
for silence, but I can't forget their innocence.
All the pain in the windows, interior glowing,
no restful gaze, no God that you ever heard,
and you keep socializing like an amateur:
you keep repeating your dreams. This is
the rough streak, a series of troubled sensations.
Are you ready to lie? I'm ready to lie and keep
lying. *Are you ready to fear?* I'm not prepared
to be afraid. Your voice is a tonic, interrogator,
it's a celebration. Mayhem even looks so good
on you; it looks like privilege and dishonor.
You need to remember I have been watching you
for centuries, precisely why
I'm so tired and winded and hungry.

Evangelical

Because it has always been it shall remain thus,
sanctification just part of the ongoing episode
about the loss of faith,
which suggests it will involve tears and scarves,
scarred retinas, dangling corneas,
and statuary the housekeeper dusts with a flower.

We hope this does not frighten you much,
escorting you into the unlocked chambers.
Let me assure you we have spent many hours strolling.
Your hand is cold. This is normal.
To your right is a dream; to your left, a mirage.
Your eyes seem troubled. We expect this.

Have you ever despised yourself over the cause
of a riddle? Or started in the middle?
Let me assure you we dream disunion and regret.
And I intend to tell you a host of anecdotes—
But I must return to staring from this misbegotten porch
at the steel sections and long and short tubing

the factory next door has assembled, thinking of the future.
If you wish, we will begin again later.

II

The Black Pants

There is absolutely no sign
of a struggle. A pair of black pants
in the road that was not
in the road yesterday at this time,
six A.M. Its zipper

is to the cobblestone. Its absent
legs are spread. It has been run over.
It's getting run over right now.
I cannot tell if these are the pants
of a man or the pants of a woman.

There hasn't been a murder
in this town for thirteen months.
Ice remains from the ice storm.
My Ford Ranger will not turn over.
At this time, the bare trees are still.

The Black Pants, Day 2

Today there is little difference
between cobblestone and the black pants.
No one has come to retrieve them
saying, "I've been looking all over
for these. Here is your reward."

If I had not known yesterday that this
blackness turned gray from black
was a simple pair of black pants,
I wouldn't know what to call it today.
If my neighbor sees what filth

has been left on our pristine street,
she will walk over in her orthopedic shoes,
pick up the black pants with the end of a stick
as if it's oozing blood or pus.
It will be like a flag. She will be proud.

The Black Pants, Evening, Day 3

The baby is in his crib. He is
winding down like a carnival
preparing to leave for the next town.
Now I finally have some time
to write about the black pants.

But I don't know what to say
about the black pants.
If love was involved, it seems
to me a good way to express it
or denounce it is to throw

one's pants from a speeding car.
And if there was a murder,
where is the body? Where is
the body? Where is the body
the pair of black pants fits?

The Black Pants, Day 4

All month it is cold in this town.
Even the sun we discussed
with the cook in the Mexican restaurant
rarely warms this town.
The black pants have nothing to do

with the sun. The fat crows
from the Oakland Cemetery
have nothing to do with the black pants,
and everything to do with the sun.
Angels weren't involved. Maybe

the Mafia was. The black pants
are covered with so much gravel
from the street today, but they are
still the black pants. The window
is so cold my tongue would stick.

The Black Pants, Evening, Day 5

Because I am an ass, not a breast
man, I can love you with
all my heart. "I'll come right to bed.
I just need to finish this poem."
"Yes, I'm still writing about

the pair of black pants in the middle
of the street in this town that
you hate in the middle of the country."
"No, actually I think it's awful;
and yes, it makes my heart race."

"Don't fall asleep because
I'm gonna climb into that
big bed with you Valentine
and nibble on them high cheekbones."
"But first, listen to what I said about us."

The Black Pants, Day 6

Someone shot to death on the morning news,
but not here in this town.
So sad, so sad. I considered
the black pants this morning
as I pulled on my tan slacks,

and in my pickup that finally
chirped then started with a roar
like relief, I did not run over
the black pants as I left home.
Don't run over the black pants.

As the mother of seven sons
said when I shut off the shop's lights,
not knowing she was still browsing,
"Don't worry. I can see in the dark."
Don't run over the black pants.

The Black Pants, Day 7

Farewell, black pants. Whoever
took you away must have needed you
for something I can only guess.
I think I know, it was a man
in a black car who stopped, opened

his door, leaned to grab the black pants.
Or my neighbor threw away the black pants,
her name is Marie. She has a good heart,
successful sons. I am tired today.
I must rest. This small house is a mess

of plants, antiques, tasseled lamps
like tentacles hanging from the walls,
hanging from the shelves. This is the day
even the dead rest, the murdered,
the ones dead before the confusion, the black pants.

This is the day one can wear

the pants one chooses. Or none.

Not My Body; Your Body

Why, the life you led,
misery, torture,
hitchhiking and motorcycling
so lovely on the back
of the Sportster
that doesn't stall
or explode into
shrapnel and burnt glue
now as prayer unmasks
the menacing face
of the rider you sat behind,

how come you never got
a tattoo or received
any potent blemish
we could spend
our sleepless nights
examining, and then—
one night to the next
like fatigued gypsies—
dab it away
with chemicals
on a dull sponge,
like common labor,
permanently?

Not Your Body; My Body

1
Measuring my wrist
is another way I've found
to pass time.
Not with a tape measure.
Eyeballing its receding girth.

2
Or call up Ed or Tom or Scott.
Or one of the Joes or Mikes,
or Angie or Susie or Mary or Nancy,
or Michaela, or Martinez . . .

3
So climb the stairs and look out the window.
If it's frozen shut,
go down for a pan of hot water?
Shoot the doe
who stands in the shade
by the woodpile?
Uncle Pasta would
with a 30-30,
"toughest son-of-a-bitch I know,"
given name, *Geno,*
shoot it through the window
then begin to regret . . .
He's killed a hundred deer—

4
But go tell one
of his three brothers
how it felt dragging
this one down to the river,
the doe sniffing round
the breadcrumbs
by the first outbuilding? . . .

5
The items
on my list include take care
of the creeping guilt.
Apologize to the neighbor
for the tire tracks.
Stop daydreaming about death.

6
I remember the attack
of nerves I had
at the restaurant,
the waiters
arguing with the cooks
after closing.
The lobby lights hot and red.
The pennies red in the fountain.

7
No one wants to hear
my dream, not even
the one with three taut ropes
around my ankles, hips, chest,
if you aren't in it

8
My current style
is this fair talent,
disappearance—
even milling around,
even right beside you.

9
I'll be telling you
a litany of my surgeries one day too.
So you'll know
with a long glance at your gold watch
to break away,
so you'll know
not to touch me.

Poem Beginning with a Line from James Merrill

Above my desk, whirring and self-important
(picture I own that gives me small hope)
twelve Indian warriors ascend to Heaven, to Mother.

Even the slightest brushstroke is a warrior,
the one who has gone the farthest of all twelve
rendered right before battle, or just after.

I will never know who they were: in one poem
I killed the unknown artist Daniel Long Soldier,
typed him into menial labor in Heaven,

granted him some hours on Sunday for painting—
after that he didn't return my calls, letters, faxes.
Why did I do that, kill a living man? *Art?*

So these warriors remain twelve men in their era,
one on a white horse, one freezing and bundled,
twelve trying to leave this place for that,

here for there. I cannot see their faces.
I cannot tell if they'll ever be successful.
They struggle: one rising from deep gray water,

one brushed lightly as a man who owns nothing . . .
I've lied again: I killed the artist Long Soldier
because he didn't return my offer, my begging.

I wanted us to collaborate: he would paint;
and I would write as he painted. So simple,
so pure. You in the corner bent to your canvas;

me at my oak desk tapping the shrill keys;
and the symphony's conductor on FM Elsewhere
standing on his sled whipping his beat dogs.

I didn't know then that Long Soldier must hate me.
I have never talked with him. Above my desk,
my painting (his painting) was stolen from him

by Leo Wounded Arrow one rainy night
in Lincoln, Nebraska. I was living with them
out there "on the street" (or thought I was).

Later that night, Leo asked to touch me, just touch,
I didn't have to move or do anything to him.
The warriors above my desk who aspire to Heaven

cannot look back or down on us, Daniel and Leo,
wherever you are right now, painting or drinking.
The Superinformation Highway is in the paper again.

Workers are laying those thin clear cables.
Any day one syllable will summon all I can imagine.
I thought together we would become great artists

of struggle. When Leo said that, I closed my eyes:
like a pack of eels through a deep sound's reefs,
it wasn't black enough, what I couldn't see.

The painting above my desk is unfinished.
The face on the white moon that is Mother is mine.

Industrialism

Out of my way, says the sunlight.
Excuse me, says her wake-to-music.
O where O where can my baby be?
the singer sings.
She wants to be located in many minds.
The industrialism of her garden in winter,
its patient captivity, the scrape
of shovel and ice pick, spread of salt and sand.
The industrialism of her smile, strong jaw
dissolving as I dug deeper in the box of photos,
all alone in her mother's house, snooping.
She needs her teeth to tear into something fresh
each day. Therefore she cannot understand
the bluebird, immune to commands.
If it sings, why would she need to bring a book
to the beach to relax, caressed by the trickle
of waves and the warm industrialism
of worn rock, with maybe one slow raft?
The industrialism as she drives down the street
with all of you, neighbors, citizens, she hopes
you're happy and blessed. When you
breathe together the industrialism of your
breathing, your most unkind phrases
knotted in a scarf of dried tears.
And of forgiveness, the industrialism of rage,
of watching her, learning how to sleep soundly.

Still Life in a Hangar with a Lion and a Woman

Lion's in its cage resting
beside the Cessna, speckless, tested out.
The trapeze artist kneels

in the corner, weeping,
holding the broken in two
and some shards cut

glass vase, and says over
and over, "This is the last straw,
the last," the glass in the light,

its reflection shrill to mute,
there is no pain like mine,
none, and take it away,

far away, into hills
atop green lush squares, into
tomorrow like a cross suspended,

with greeting birdsong
and the bliss of thrown rice
warm in the palm,

cold in the white breeze
as it falls sharply
on their faces,

on their luxurious cheeks.

Manx

When Miles Davis slows down
in the middle of "Spanish Key"—

on the bolted, oak door
my cat's paws are brushes on cymbals—

does she dream of cutting my throat
in the room where I type,

slender Sphinx, black over white?—
sometimes when I hear her

scratching I think back to boys
who buried stray cats neck-high—

disappeared into that quicksand,
alert fright on their monkey faces—

I think of those boys firing
up an old lawnmower: blue oil cloud,

and then—when I consider my own
selfish brutality something

rigid runs through me, as if
my body's a pond dredged for

a drowned fisherman—"a Manx
has an internal vestigial tail"—

her name is Charlotte: *good kitty,
good kitty* . . . my pet by marriage—

she, the red sofa, the antiques—
sometimes when I'm typing

I let her in and she sits on the edge
of my desk and licks herself—

sometimes when I finish
typing I look out the window—

streetlight lighting my car:
I think, how many payments left?

how much gas in the tank?—
wind lashing the bushes—

and the rain is a twenty-one-gun salute,
but I think I'll just walk out there,

here I go, watch me, so long, I loved you—
I loved you too—

Artistic

Not what your mother
hangs on her white walls,

what your crazed uncle
Andre hangs on his hazel

walls, what the neighbors say
about Andre, joyous

as he is on the sauce
and melancholy

when he's not, walking
the streets late at night

like a man without
shoulders, like a man

without arms, without
a neck, without limbs.

Girl, they're calling you
artistic, and I wouldn't

let them, not here in
this school, not in

these halls, not so early
in the morning, not

so late in this impossible,
scathed and muddy day.

Almost Motionless on Nob Hill

The pizza-man came and went, two-dollar tip.
Cool Hand Luke's on WTBS.
More than enough slices for both of us.
Any blessing tonight, any *touching*?
Will terror be what forgives me?
She washed her face, she looks like
a mannequin who owns one wig.
Incandescence, light in four movements,
a green spineless A in mist tops Transamerica.
—Just before we arrived I was hoping
for relief, someone to despise; my eye
encountered unstrung feisty syllabics
of hate, another prayer, answered;
another nightmare, afraid to wake.
I wash me away, flush from a scene.
Who would pray so hard to be *unfree*?
Pizza-man handed me a wet pizza box.
Finally we had decided—come
to terms—paused, looked each other
in the eye . . . because she wanted her black
olive, I ordered my pepperoni on half.
—Valet grinned us in the first day
over the curb, big green rented sedan,
our luggage on wheels, her hair, *up* . . .
Concierge rang—two knocks, pizza-man.
"It's not my honeymoon," I said. Never
have I slept in a hotel sumptuous as this,
airport closed two whole days, fog—
and I'll never check into this place again,
so long as I'm the one paying.

Ennui from the Mezzanine

Concerning light: promises exchanged
and we're holding hands again,
a medium light in this medium day,
no undotted celestial range.

We watched the dipping crane up close
from our eighth floor corner suite,
humpbacked ascension of materials,
arcing birdsong, another clear enough day.

I notice so many of you seem so *pleased*.
One needs to learn how to proceed
through fog, high water, conflagrations,
the noxious fibers of our well-sewn clothes,

and don't tell you believe you are Jesus
dying for their hearty sins, even when
they threaten torture—water, shock, bamboo.
What we own, we own, we own.

The seasons are changing, while you wait.
Open the window a crack. That's enough.

IV

Accidental Gunshot Wound

The remedy is a long walk in City Park
where you can still see the edges
of the newly mown swipes.
The remedy is *running* not *jogging*.
The remedy is exhaustion then lying still.
Charred walls and nests of wiring exposed
and two bullet holes in the foyer—
the remedy is sit still, let the phone jangle,
the machine will pick it up,
911 with their routine verification—
it couldn't happen here again like last time—
turn on the TV and you are not mad again:
the anchorwoman whose teeth are placards,
she's a slogan, the weatherman points and smiles.
The remedy is striving toward clarity,
open-eyed apprehension of mystery,
admitting to the fountain all your wishes were lies.
—When we were together the last time
and the trees were glad open throats,
and our mouths where our subtle tongues hid,
and our legs, which were bruised all over,
and our arms, thin as refugees',
and our chests, maps of destructed city-states
stenciled across them—
the remedy is a significant union like ours.
The remedy is being apart from the one you love.
Maybe Maria swings on the white porchswing
because she loves watching us walk past.
Maybe Maria is the remedy,
even though her smile is twisted and foul.
Maria's father has always been away:
the remedy is ongoing, furious travel.
The remedy is sitting in the cellar hating

heroes, walking upstairs and switching on
the vacuum, staring at the cracked plaster,
boiling water, switching channels,
falling in love with another image of beauty,
drinking coffee from a big-handled mug.
We thought the remedy was *sit still*.
The remedy is go out into the noise;
the remedy is the indecipherable noise,
cars in regular patterns, polite drivers . . .
This is a town that needs to have its way.
Don't think you go unnoticed walking through.
You are just another clumsy pedestrian
who has escaped his pained quiet.
The remedy is the clarity of your name
rising out of the foregrounded noise.
Don't you see, *amigo*? The remedy is
this city unsaying your cruel name.

Dinner Poem

The scariest part of any feast is dessert.
You see your twisted reflection in the tray.
The whole time my legs under the tablecloth
have been crooked and cocked.
He is telling a story about Yakima,
about the railroad, about a certain streetcar
he engineered down the parade route.
The many legs of the women arrive.
They must have faces.
I have spent most of my life looking down.
I found a dime once, but when I didn't
stoop and pick it up I had to hear
a story of the Great Depression, etc.
The dialogue hammers. It makes you
feel dumb inside. You are still, you focus,
Om, you are centered and certainly privileged,
even as somewhere some man staggers
who used to wear your coat,
size forty-two long, gray, two buttons,
the one you wear to every dinner.
The one he sells to a careful stranger.

Gossip

The gossips lean on the fence like convicts,
cigarette smoke skywriting their fatigue,
Forest Lawn Cemetery like a medieval stage
in the background.
They talk tomatoes, lust,
Reverend, hosiery,
picnic, cancer,
grandkids, light bills.
Their sons are away at war.
Their sons, recently, were here
climbing out of bedroom windows,
jumping then disappearing like deer
back to once secret shores.
What about the daughters
who wait, who have given up?
Their sweethearts
never walked them three steps
up to the porch, hands cupping their hips,
or opened doors like attendants.
Now they board planes with no seats,
sleep on sharp welds.
This is a short history of photography,
photos in apron pockets
or stared at through the steam
rising from cups of coffee.
The daughters-in-law,
at home with the beautiful children,
have faces gossips cry for
when they aren't crying for where
their lives have been pushed
for twenty-five years,
lives like their mothers'
and all mothers ever since
their stories of true love
were translated by the soft strong hands
of the fathers.

Epithalamium

We were down to change, walking.
Stopping inside those brilliant casinos
to insert our last silver dollars,
to pull their smudged, sprung levers,

calling out our faint luck.
We had been married the night before.
We woke up in Caesars Palace
on a red double sofa that did not

make me feel I was waking in a puddle
of my own blood, or hers.
It was late, in that chapel.
The minister kept adjusting his pants,

asking us our names. That night
we walked the Glitter Gulch,
husband and wife, I think I said,
"I'm a poet," or "I want to be a poet,"

or "Does beauty sometimes terrify you?"
or "I feel strange about what beauty is not."
I held her hand. For many blocks
I could not look her in the eye.

There was a loud learned silence
in the middle of the desert.
What I meant to say is that we
must always stay three steps ahead

of the rational, and that baby, dear,
child—whatever I will learn to call
you well—it can run a man and his bride
down on their knees in the gravel.

The Politics of Marriage

The man who sells encyclopedias has twenty-six wives.

The man who sells dreams, e.g.,
You can make a fortune, yes, you,
had four wives.

He admires me for nothing I can think of.
I long to touch his dead brides,
but only if they boast of my technique
over the phone
as I open an old bottle from his cellar.

The scholar takes a barrio of books
for his bride. When he's violent,
the city doesn't listen;
chased down a dirt road, his cries
drown under the wheels of a borrowed wagon.

He curses the day-old bread,
the crumbs of wisdom in his frugal beard.

I'm thinking of the Russian novelists
I hated once for their productivity,
and loved too late.

My old friends are finally
admitting their love for girls
who need them, who make them happy.

I don't receive those invitations in the mail.

The postman loves his wife too much:
it's in his brisk walk.

I open what he leaves for me.
Need is never mentioned. Nor is *desire*.

"You want to fall in love,"
Bazarov says,
"and you can't love. That's where
your unhappiness lies."

He was talking about himself.

At the end, he dies, neither fearing
the afterlife nor at peace with the world,
as pets often die, in a child's arms.

He was a scientist. He knew everything
about the machinery of the body.

He was talking about his aorta.
As if *broken heart* could never
appeal to his methods.

Taxonomy

In this faulty taxonomy
I keep mixing lovers of devastation
with tellers of riddles.

One twists his wedding ring as he thinks;
one weeds round a grave-marker.

I keep confusing pain and wisdom,
craving and love, hope and fatigue
and tenderness.

I should've paid more attention in school.
Just think where I'd be now.
Instead, it is as if nothing ever happened
there, rows of tiny desks, long-handled

hairy combs inside.

Love Poem

The rain was the reason we didn't hike very far,
attendant lightning, fireworks fizzling.
After exhilaration, detumescence, celebrant.
All the fatigued shucking not to mention jiving

into the intoxication chamber, secret sharer . . .
Come into the chemical rooms . . . mixtures, oxidizers.
Eat what ails you, kill what irks you, inappropriate
punning on lift-off, separation, take-off, autopilot.

There's old glass in the rotting window frame.
What about the *widow's fame*?
This is the sound of many sounds.
This is what she looks like holding forth no further:

metallic leggings, subsonic thoughts, rouge,
the particles and fragments of her, and I have been
meaning to tell you—I have meant to say so much
is happening on the mountain, on this precipice . . .

Substandard camping, how we keep filling a boot
with water, the ground with feces, our mouths
with homemade pie—caramel, rhubarb, meringue—
malice with nurturing words, with tales of forgiveness.

Who does a girl have to fuck to get a drink around here?
The first full sentence I heard her say, interrogatory,
a cliché, sure, but triteness within a dream of thin glassware.
Before later when it was momentarily *real love*,

hot and bright, which is dimmer now in comparison,
in memory—half-moon cut in the old trapdoor,
you keep me neither sated nor kind.

Oceanic

Maybe if this weren't
the language I think
and feel in all day
every day, curse in,
whisper in when I
make love to my wife
in the morning still
controlled by the moon
before the baby
wakes. If language were like
the powerboat I fear
but captain one week
each summer, scanning
port, starboard, leaning
to spit in the wake,
and if it were something
I could come to about
once a week, like laundry,
like overwhelming doubt,
then could I tell you
about the windmills,
and would you see windmills
turn in the wind? I think
I'll let my wife captain
the boat next summer when
we go to Cliff Island
to visit her rich parents
who pour me strong drinks
and ask me questions
such as "Who is the muse
of your poetry?" There must be
worlds beneath the waves . . .
I'll tell her I just want

to watch the islands—
like dishes a waiter
lifts from the table—
spin by me . . . And still,
and yet, therefore, because,
and in spite of this
life of mine, somehow
it's not about language.
Sometimes, what happens
outside my door, like what
the neighbors are doing
right now, March Thirtieth,
ten P.M., thirty degrees,
is the hardest thing
to remind myself to tell you.

On Fog

This island's forgotten the name
of its wealthiest man.

Winking at the gone sun,
our compass is a glass eye
floating in a dumb head.

—But just try to keep us on
forty-five degrees and I'll watch
for reefs, for other boats, for land,

but both of us should
listen for the bell buoy

and watch for land's ghost physique
under no sun, no stars yet that we know.

The afterthoughts this island would utter,
as its twenty-two lights blacken,
after its goodnight prayers,
one stray wave licking the highest rock,
are the names of its poorest men,
and what they owe, and to whom.

—You're the wealthiest man's daughter,
his little girl. Ours is one of his five boats
he'll miss. But not for long. He'll walk
to the modest hearth for his silver candlestick
holders to hurl at the white flake of mooring.

You love some version of him, and me,
you say, and you know this bay,
these charts, better than he or I;

What thou lov'st well shall not
be reft from thee,
what thou lovest well remains.

If I'm man all dressed up
in his coffin;

If you're his widow who weeps
and rearranges the bouquets.

The Near-Wreck

Our bodies
inhabiting this world of collisions—
    no good excuses
or lives left. Only frail gestures
    of renewal. Or become
one of us who hides indoors
    the rest of my life
watching the televised universe
    grovel and gloat?

You remember almost dying with me,
    don't you?
On many curves, under the sun,
    in various cars . . .
On River Road we got out
    and you touched the tires,
hot, from three-sixties—
    the girls in the backseat
cold,
    shaking and crying
together, their teeth as white
    as piano keys then,
decrescendo,
    da capo . . .

After the near-wreck:
the corn stalks monumental
    and doomed
in the cold, hard ground,
    the screaming of our names
over the onrush
    of our dismissal
of nature.
    Who could hear?

Having been born and raised
   just miles from this scene,
intending to die
   brightly and soundly,
left to be found
   by some fatigued driver.

"In addition to the terrors of absence, what's in the margins, the *white space*?"

—"Unhousedness," couch abandoned road-side,
mantle-piece balanced on the armrest.

—The runner stands, turns around,
his locomotion a hole, then a grave,
lilies settling on the curved coffin.

—She looks up. They *both* laugh—
arms at their sides quaver, momentarily a light
in his eyes that's Godlike
and it's *cobalt*, she thinks.

—Ideas gleaned from travel never reported.
Her song, *a cappella* . . .
how free? so free *(un-
rendered)*.

—In the tree a bird lands, gentle friend,
nature and text, prayer and meaning.

—Some dreamers grow up and out of this;
last staring thought before the dreamer snores.

—An old man who reads a poem to practice dying.
He reads a poem to practice dying,
he crosses out many of the words.

Rhapsodic

If I don't think at least one beautiful thought
lying in our bed, this book a rain-heavy tent
on my chest (Larry Brown's *Fay*),
—and she's asleep upright . . . lawn ornament,
staked, my formal bird—
the rain that once was upset petals
now the thorny remains of stems—
then let the sickened dreamlife loose,
memory's germs anthropomorphic, free,
each pushing a boulder with my tired eyes
taped on it up the hill in the sunlight
that pours out of a larger face's jaw and teeth
and shakes a bit what is loveliest, shattered.

—Because what passes for my best thinking
in this violent town is usually its violence
and partially so; but the bare truth (and pardon
the expression) is even lukewarm violence
reddens some cheeks and mine; and I'm tired
of weeping and fearing its surplus . . . this is
another reason I move seat-to-seat-to-seat
on the bus, and look downward, dismiss heroes,
and whistle for noise or solace or both.

But if I am to begin thinking of the violent
as beautiful, and my own downcast origin
and myself as another attractive enough
item in its thick catalogue, where to find
this combination but in the other kingdom
which is holier and always was
but will not allow my restless tampering,
my heavy-footed steps same as an old man
who sighs in the dark must remember as his gait
each time he leaves his house for town?

—So here's another catalogue: this one contains
mist as its background, and how the zero
was created, colliding numbers like faults
that create a crevasse—which is a whisper—
and the music of mist and forgetting combining
with my titillation of "jumping off"
(and our disastrous multiple disunions)
now transformed into this painless greeting
not to her or you but to three harmonious birds,
none of which I can name in my greening backyard.

—And another: how she brings joy to her
discontinuity . . . and in the open spaces where wind
stops to strategize onwardness, we stare at numerals
on top of numerals, it seems, with our affectations
to keep us warm at twilight—to keep me smiling—
with rivaled and sporadic ascent. But ascent's
no longer the only aim (and victory's the hardest
one to bleed out, but it must be bled outward
onto the mop and then all the linen in the closet) . . .

and there are other mysteries, many of which are hollow
and beautiful both, later to be examined and named,
but for now say, "Such as the next one,
as it arrives and is gone too soon but left a trail
that's ribbon-like—many ribbons, actually—
and it smells like the air on the shore of the pond,
like something that passed through a life,
and you would fish here all day and be glad."

Red Herring

Buzzing reliquaries in a swampland chapel.
Eternalized maquettes on a storeroom shelf.
Please don't tell me how many nights we spent
walking and it just happened to start to rain.

Vibrations and hallucinations were twin sisters
to me then. The smell of realism under the stairs,
the pandemonium of free fall, psychology,
chart reading, crypt-building, glad-handing . . .

I was always talking about struggle against doom.
I still am. It seems you have been listening.
But are you happy here, are you satisfied yet?
In Maine, in Vermont, when you enter Canada

the air is so fresh. You said, Remember. *Breathe.*

Decade

The decade being sung to you backward,
is this why you cover your mouth when the subject
is sorrow? You were trying hard to enact
an apocalyptic stammer in your walk
but discovered many of your friends were annoyed
and talking together about the alteration of your ethos.
This was before the advent of your enmeshed spirituality.
You had decided on odd jobs as a vocation
and a weekly poker game. I am telling not showing
which I realize is more true to my experience.
She invited my wife to Vietnam for three weeks
to pick up her baby and fill out the papers.
Her baby is beautiful with a Polish middle name
same as her father's. I love to go to the ocean—
whenever I get the chance—I don't fish, sail, kayak.
The maître d' made me feel like an orphan again.
There is fatigue in the jowls of the organ.
The organist is tired, too, and waiting for the moment
that had been promised. I have so many stories
you would not believe anyway such as the one
about your hero. She smiles and it is like the memory
of crepe paper at a child's party; it is like the breaking
of the piñata. I am the one who hires the salespersons
for the boiler room. When I am not at work I juggle
the mundane expectancies of my position as father
and husband. Ask me before you decide to live
a double life and the committee will meet to make sure
you have the goods. The seasons are not fitting
into the paradigm anymore, and I'm listening
to the music I had sworn off, I'm sneaking cough syrup,
I'm dreaming in Jungian. This poem was dictated
by a family of nine, three of whom rode to school
in the fully opened trunk. I watched

the fire in Texas on TV at the Deadwood Bar,
a favorite stop for morning drinkers who quote Nietzsche.
Later, the balding bartender barked—I woke
from my daydream. We sent the kids out with cookies
to cheer the aged. We dispatched the older ones
with frozen Margaritas to make the teenagers happy.
A transistor radio in the Smithsonian plays Buddy Holly;
we saw the Ruby Slippers. Mark Rothko came down
from Heaven to paint in my blue book. A blue book
is what you need in college and into which you write
the long indecipherable never to be read answer on your final.
This is the decade whistling its favorite tune while strolling.
A friend called every day for three weeks when I was sad:
I painted my apartment off-black in the nude. I can settle
for gardening as a sufficient non-confrontational topic
while you finish your broccoli chicken and hot tea.
It would be grown up of us to refrain from sighing.
There is a 57 Chevy in the parking lot that is not ours.

Welcome to the Neighborhood

I have not heard from a single one.
None of them has brought over a casserole
covered with tin foil or an invitation
in a font as prepossessing as *Arial*.

Is it because I have been dead now
for just under two hundred years,
after having had over ten thousand seizures
and three dozen operations you are welcome

to peruse in detail in *The New England Journal
of Medicine*? My neighbors are Serena, Holly,
Dermot—Serena has two cats. Through keen
attention and penetrating insight I've learned

Holly is a dancer, Dermot played rugby
and he inherited a collection of steins,
balanced on his windowsills like the Changing
of the Guard. We don't know each other yet,

but we have so much in common,
alone at breakfast, hunched in corner booths,
limping home with crumbs in our wigs.
Pacing the linoleum, numbering the planets,

shooting the presidents, begging the hydrants for mercy.

photo by Helene Quigley

Steve Langan was born in Milwaukee in 1965. His graduate
degree is from the University of Iowa Writers' Workshop, where
he received the James Michener Fellowship, and his poems
have been published in *DoubleTake, The Kenyon Review, Chicago
Review, Columbia: A Journal of Literature and Art,* and *Witness.*
He lives in Omaha with his wife and son.

New Issues Poetry & Prose

Editor, Herbert Scott

James Armstrong, *Monument in a Summer Hat*
Michael Burkard, *Pennsylvania Collection Agency*
Anthony Butts, *Fifth Season*
Gladys Cardiff, *A Bare Unpainted Table*
Lisa Fishman, *The Deep Heart's Core Is a Suitcase*
Joseph Featherstone, *Brace's Cove*
Robert Grunst, *The Smallest Bird in North America*
Mark Halperin, *Time as Distance*
Myronn Hardy, *Approaching the Center*
Edward Haworth Hoeppner, *Rain Through High Windows*
Janet Kauffman, *Rot* (fiction)
Josie Kearns, *New Numbers*
Maurice Kilwein Guevara, *Autobiography of So-and-so: Poems in Prose*
Ruth Ellen Kocher, *When the Moon Knows You're Wandering*
Steve Langan, *Freezing*
Lance Larsen, *Erasable Walls*
David Dodd Lee, *Downsides of Fish Culture*
Deanne Lundin, *The Ginseng Hunter's Notebook*
Joy Manesiotis, *They Sing to Her Bones*
David Marlatt, *A Hog Slaughtering Woman*
Sarah Messer, *Bandit Letters*
Paula McLain, *Less of Her*
Malena Mörling, *Ocean Avenue*
Julie Moulds, *The Woman with a Cubed Head*
Marsha de la O, *Black Hope*
C. Mikal Oness, *Water Becomes Bone*
Elizabeth Powell, *The Republic of Self*
Margaret Rabb, *Granite Dives*
Rebecca Reynolds, *Daughter of the Hangnail*
Martha Rhodes, *Perfect Disappearance*
Beth Roberts, *Brief Moral History in Blue*
John Rybicki, *Traveling at High Speeds*
Mary Ann Samyn, *Inside the Yellow Dress*